The Intention of Patriarch Bodhidharma's Coming from the West

The Intention of Patriarch Bodhidharma's Coming from the West

by the Venerable Master Hsuan Hua

Translated and published by the
Buddhist Text Translation Society
Dharma Realm Buddhist University
Dharma Realm Buddhist Association
Burlingame, California U.S.A.
2000

The Intention of Patriarch Bodhidharma's Coming from the West
English edition
Compiled from lectures by the Venerable Master Hsuan Hua.

Published by:
Buddhist Text Translation Society
1777 Murchison Drive
Burlingame, California 94010-4504

© 2000   Buddhist Text Translation Society
            Dharma Realm Buddhist University
            Dharma Realm Buddhist Association

First bilingual Chinese/English edition 2000
First English edition 2000

09 08 07 06 05 04 03 02 01 00   10 9 8 7 6 5 4 3 2 1

Printed in Taiwan, R.O.C.

Addresses of the Dharma Realm Buddhist Association branches are
listed at the back of this book.

Library of Congress Cataloging-in-Publication Data

Hsuan Hua, 1908-
    [Ta-mo-tsu-shih hsi lai i. English]
    The intention of patriarch Bodhidharma's coming from the West / by the Venerable Master
Hsuan Hua ; translated by the Buddhist Text Translation Society, Dharma Realm Buddhist
University, Dharma Realm Buddhist Association.
        p. cm.
    ISBN 0-88139-315-0 (pbk : alk. paper)
    1. Bodhidharma, 6th cent.-Anecdotes. 2. Zen Buddhism-Anecdotes. I. Buddhist Text Translation
Society. II. Dharma Realm Buddhist University. III. Dharma Realm Buddhist Association. IV. Title.

BQ9299.B627 H75 2000
294.3'927'092—dc21

                                                        00-058537

The Eight Guidelines
of the Buddhist Text Translation Society

1. A volunteer must free himself or herself from the motives of personal fame and profit.

2. A volunteer must cultivate a respectful and sincere attitude free from arrogance and conceit.

3. A volunteer must refrain from aggrandizing his or her work and denigrating that of others.

4. A volunteer must not establish himself or herself as the standard of correctness and suppress the work of others with his or her fault-finding.

5. A volunteer must take the Buddha-mind as his or her own mind.

6. A volunteer must use the wisdom of Dharma-Selecting Vision to determine true principles.

7. A volunteer must request Virtuous Elders in the ten directions to certify his or her translations.

8. A volunteer must endeavor to propagate the teachings by printing Sutras, Shastra texts, and Vinaya texts when the translations are certified as being correct.

The Intention of Patriarch Bodhidharma's Coming from the West

When conditions in China were ripe, Master Bodhidharma went there.

The emperor failed to recognize him; his time had not yet arrived.

But Shen Guang knelt for nine years at Bear's Ear Mountain

And became Hui Ke after the snow was stained by his severed arm.

The Master transmitted the mind seal of the Great Dharma

To him as the Second Patriarch, continuing the wise traditions.

Poisoned six times, the Master was never harmed in the least.

Carrying a single shoe, he returned to the West, never to be forgotten.

by Venerable Master Hua, November 15, 1983

3

Originally I came to this land

To transmit Dharma and save deluded beings.

One flower, blooming with five petals,

Will bear fruit naturally.

I have often told you that when Patriarch Bodhidharma first went to China, he found it truly difficult to convert the Chinese people.

Patriarch Bodhidharma
Comes from the West to China

Bodhidharma—"Bodhi" meaning enlightened and "Dharma" meaning the teachings—was the Twenty-eighth Patriarch in India. Why didn't he stay in India and be a Patriarch there? Why did he go to China? Well, previously Shakyamuni Buddha made a prediction that from the Twenty-eighth Patriarch on, the Great Vehicle teaching should go to China. Thus it happened that Patriarch Bodhidharma sailed from India to China.

Buddhism Seems to Be in China,
Yet It Really Is Not

At that time, the Buddhadharma seemed to exist in China, but it really did not. It was as if it were and yet weren't there. That is because the work being done was superficial. There were few who recited Sutras, investigated the Sutra texts, or explained the Sutras, and virtually no one bowed repentance ceremonies. Ordinary scholars regarded Buddhism as a field of study and engaged in debates and discussions about it.

But the principles in the Sutras should be cultivated! However, nobody was cultivating. Why not? People were afraid of suffering. No one truly meditated. Well, there was Venerable Patriarch Zhi, who practiced meditation and attained the Five Eyes. But most people feared suffering and didn't cultivate. No one seriously investigated Chan and sat in meditation, just like you people now who sit in meditation for a while until your legs begin to hurt. When their legs began to ache, they would wince and fidget and then gently unbend and rub them. People are just people, and everyone avoids suffering as much as possible. That's the way it was then; that's the way it is now. That's called Buddhadharma seeming to be there but not really being there.

When the Disciples First Came,
They Met with Difficulty

Before Patriarch Bodhidharma himself went to China, he sent two of his disciples there first. Who would have thought that when they got to China they would be totally ostracized and bullied? Those two disciples, named Fo Tuo and Ye She, were Indians who went to China to transmit the Sudden Teaching Dharma Door of the Chan School that advocates seeing the nature and becoming a Buddha, and which does not abide in language. At that time in China another Indian monk named Bodhiruchi was aware that these two monks had also come from India to explain the Chan School. Chan belongs to the Great Vehicle Teaching, but Bodhiruchi explained the Tripitaka Teaching, which belongs to the Small Vehicle. For that reason, Bodhiruchi got all other monks to join together to ostricize these two Indian monks. No matter what they said, no one would listen. No matter where they went, everyone ignored them. Deciding that the situation was meaningless, they left. That is how these two disciples of Patriarch Bodhidharma came to leave the western capitol of Changan.

The Hand Makes a Fist;
The Fist Makes a Hand

On their way out they passed by Lu Mountain where they met the Great Master Zhiyuan (Huiyuan), who promoted the practice of reciting the Buddha's name. He himself recited the Buddha's name all the time. Well, they went to pay their respects to Great Master Yuan. Venerable Yuan said to them, "What Dharma do you two monks from India transmit that causes people to pay you so little respect?"

Fo Tuo and Ye She both extended their hands. They probably knew very little Chinese. Extending their hands, they said, "The hand makes a fist, and the fist makes a hand. Isn't that fast?"

Master Yuan replied, "Very fast!"

"Bodhi and affliction," they said, "are just that fast!"

At that moment, Great Master Yuan became enlightened and said, "Ah! Bodhi and affliction basically are not different! Bodhi is affliction and affliction is Bodhi." Having gained such an understanding, Great Master Yuan made abundant offerings to Fo Tuo and Ye She. Shortly thereafter, the two died on the same day, in the same place. Their graves may still be seen at Lu Mountain.

Back in India, when Patriarch Bodhidharma learned that his two disciples had been scorned and had both died, he thought, "I will go there myself to have a look." Thereupon he went to China.

Patriarch Bodhidharma saw that the roots of the Great Vehicle Buddhadharma were ripe in China and knew that he should take the Great Vehicle Dharma there. Fearing neither the distance nor the hardship of travel, he took the Dharma there. What do you suppose it was like when he arrived in China?

Arriving First at Guangzhou,
He Is Feared by All Who See Him

Patriarch Bodhidharma went to Guangzhou first. When children there saw such a dark and bearded Indian, they surrounded him as if he were performing a street show. At that time the Chinese people were rather snobbish toward foreigners. They called Indians "Mo Luo Cha" (meaning devil, or devilish ghost). The Patriarch became Monk Mo Luo Cha. They even composed a rhyme that they chanted, "Devil! Devil! Skin you, I will." They wanted to skin him alive! See how Patriarch Bodhidharma was ridiculed and insulted? However, Patriarch Bodhidharma could not understand what they were saying because he did not know Chinese. He didn't speak their language and couldn't communicate verbally with them. He wanted to befriend the children in that place, but as soon as they saw Patriarch Bodhidharma, they went crazy and scattered in all directions. They dared not to be near this Mo Luo Cha. Why? They were afraid of his long beard.

Being Insulted Left and Right, He Finds Both Adults and Children Difficult to Convert

When the adults saw that children ran away from him, they suspected this Indian was a kidnapper. So they bid their children to stay away from the Patriarch. He could not even convert children; how could he convert the grown-ups? No one dared to get close to him. That was the situation in Guangzhou; no one recognized that he was a patriarch. Consequently, he did not stay long in Guangzhou and moved on to Nanjing. While traveling on foot, he was also greeted by many children who yelled, "Ah! An Indian!" and threw clods of dirt at him.

Emperor Wu of Liang
Boasts of His Own Merit and Virtue

When Patriarch Bodhidharma first arrived in Nanjing from Guangzhou, he went to convert Emperor Wu. Emperor Wu asked him, "In my whole life, I have built many temples, helped many people to leave the home-life, provided the needy with money from the national treasury, and also made vegetarian meal offerings to the Sangha. What merit and virtue have I created?" At that time, whoever left the home-life would be treated well by the Emperor, with everything including food, dwelling, and clothing provided for. As long as you were a left home person, the emperor would make offerings to you, pay reverence to you, and bow to you.

Emperor Wu was the kind of person who wanted to be number one in everything. That was why when he met Patriarch Bodhidharma, he didn't seek Dharma from him. Instead he was totally engrossed in how to win praise from the Patriarch. He wanted to inflate his ego. Concerned that the Patriarch might not know of the good deeds that he had done, such as building temples, converting monks, practicing giving, and making vegetarian meal offerings, he went ahead and pointed them out as he introduced himself to the Patriarch. He said, "You see, I have built hundreds of temples. This one and that one all house many monks whom I helped to leave the home-life. The amount of giving I have done is not small, and the number of monks I have provided for is not small. How much merit and virtue would you say I've amassed?" Basically, he was providing his own promotion campaign. He was saying, "Look at me! I am different from other emperors. I specialize in doing good deeds, creating merit and virtue. How much merit and virtue would you say I have?" He did not want to seek the Dharma for ending birth and death; instead, he wanted to boast of his own merit and virtue first.

Actually He Had
No Merit and Virtue At All

Patriarch Bodhidharma listened to Emperor Wu of Liang praising himself as if drunk on his own ego, introducing himself, boasting of his merit and virtue, advertising for himself, calling attention to his own good points, and generally lauding himself. Most people, upon hearing the Emperor's comments, would have said, "Ah! Of course you have merit and virtue! You have tremendous merit and virtue! Your merit and virtue is out of this world!" That would be most people's response. Now I ask you, would a sage ever say things just to flatter someone? But Bodhidharma was a patriarch. How could he possibly flatter and fawn? And so he replied, "Actually you have no merit and virtue. In truth, no merit and virtue at all."

Patriarch Bodhidharma originally had gone there with the idea of saving Emperor Wu of Liang. However, Emperor Wu was too conceited; he had too high an opinion of himself. Being an emperor was already something, he thought. He had built many temples, enabled many people to leave home, given away a lot of money, and made a lot of offerings to the Triple Jewel. So, he thought he had created a tremendous amount of merit and virtue. Patriarch Bodhidharma, wanting to shatter the Emperor's attachment, said that he had no merit and virtue at all.

Meeting Face-to-Face, He Misses His Chance, Failing to Recognize the Patriarch

For the Patriarch to say he had no merit and virtue was one thing, but for Emperor Wu of Liang to hear that was another, for it made him quite unhappy. From then on, the Emperor ignored Patriarch Bodhidharma. No matter what Dharma the Patriarch spoke, the Emperor refused to listen. "Why should I listen to you?" Emperor Wu's karmic obstacles were too heavy. Although Patriarch Bodhidharma came from India to become the First Patriarch of China, Emperor Wu of Liang failed to recognize him. He was face-to-face and missed his chance. The Chinese people have a saying, "Coming face-to-face, one fails to recognize the Bodhisattva Who Contemplates the Sounds of the World." Emperor Wu of Liang was face-to-face and failed to recognize the One Who Intentionally Came from the West. He did not recognize the Patriarch who came from the West. Why did Patriarch Bodhidharma want to save him? He knew that the Emperor was going to encounter some difficulty, so he wanted to help the Emperor awaken. Had Emperor Wu been able to leave home and cultivate, or to yield his throne to someone else, he could have avoided the fate of starving to death.

Causes and Conditions from a Previous Life:
He Starved a Monkey

Emperor Wu originally had deep faith in the Buddhadharma. During his time, Buddhism flourished in China. Using his power as an emperor, he built temples everywhere and promoted Buddhism. Consequently, many people came to believe in the Buddhadharma.

However, he had also created very heavy karma in a past life. What kind of a person had Emperor Wu been in the past? He had been a Bhikshu, a Buddhist monk. While that monk cultivated up in the mountains, a monkey would come every day to steal the things he planted for food and to steal the fruit from the nearby trees, such as peaches, apples, and the like. The monkey stole and ate all the fruit and most of the vegetables the monk planted. Finally one day the monk managed to trap the monkey in a cave and blocked the entrance of the cave with rocks. Basically he planned to keep the monkey in there for a couple of days and then let it out, in order to teach the monkey a lesson so that it wouldn't steal his food anymore. Who would have guessed that after blocking up the cave he would forget about it, thus causing that monkey to die of hunger!

Receiving Retribution in This Life,
He Starves to Death in the Palace

In this life, he was an emperor, and the monkey was reborn to be Hou Jing. Hou Jing led soldiers to attack Nanjing. After Nanjing was taken, he kept Emperor Wu in captivity in the palace and did not provide him with any food. He took all food away, and left the Emperor there to starve to death. In a previous life, the Emperor starved the monkey to death, and in this life the monkey starved him to death. He had to undergo that retribution.

Now before that happened, Patriarch Bodhidharma saw that the Emperor had done so many good deeds that he could have redeemed his offense with the merit and virtue created. However, to do so there must be some conditions. That's why the Patriarch was not polite to him. But the Emperor thought to himself, "I am an emperor, a great emperor, and you are only a poor monk. You come to my country and are utterly rude to me." So he alienated himself from the Patriarch. Though Patriarch Bodhidharma wanted to save him and brought forth a compassionate mind toward him, the Emperor could not accept him. Because the Emperor made no move to seek help from the Patriarch, there was nothing the Patriarch could do to help him. Thus, the Patriarch left and paid no more attention to the Emperor.

What happened as a result was that after a period of time, Emperor Wu was captured and starved to death in the palace by Hou Jing and his people. Such was the cause and effect. You all think about it. If the Emperor actually had merit and virtue, how could he have starved to death? It was because he did not have merit and virtue that he died of hunger. Patriarch Bodhidharma wanted to save him from his fate by helping him reach an awakening. What a pity that Emperor Wu of Liang's ego was so big that even Patriarch Bodhidharma could not save him.

The Heavens Rain Down Flowers;
Golden Lotuses Well Forth from the Earth

While still in Nanjing, after he left the imperial court, Patriarch Bodhidharma met the Venerable Shen Guang (Spiritual Light), who was lecturing on the Sutras. When Dharma Master Shen Guang explained the Sutras, the heavens rained down flowers, and golden lotuses welled forth from the earth. Heavenly maidens scattered blossoms, and from beneath the earth golden lotuses burst forth. Ah! What a supreme state!

The Patriarch heard about that, and so he also went to observe the Dharma assembly and listen to the Sutra lecture. By then he probably had learned some Chinese and could speak a few sentences. If on the road from Guangzhou to Nanjing, he learned one sentence a day, he would have learned ten sentences in ten days, and a hundred in a hundred days. That Patriarch was very intelligent; he did not have to study to learn Chinese, he just listened.

In Nanjing, he listened to Dharma Master Shen Guang explain a Sutra. Dharma Master Shen Guang was quite pleased by that. "Hah! See how well I lecture the Sutras? Even an Indian has come to listen! Ah! He came from so far away to listen to my lecture. How truly inconceivable!" He felt quite good about it.

The Patriarch Asks Him,
"Why Are You Explaining Sutras?"

After he finished his Sutra lecture, he was surprised when the Indian began to question him. The Patriarch asked, "Dharma Master, what are you doing?"

Dharma Master Shen Guang replied, "I am lecturing on the Sutras. You don't even know that? I thought you came to listen to the explanation of the Sutra, but it turns out you don't even know what a Sutra lecture is all about!"

Patriarch Bodhidharma asked, "Hmm. What are you doing when you lecture on the Sutras? Why explain Sutras?"

Dharma Master Shen Guang
Retorts Sarcastically

Dharma Master Shen Guang said, "Hey! What did you come here for? Don't you even know what Sutra lectures are all about? Where did you come from?"

"I came here from India."

"You come from India, and I am here explaining the Buddhist scriptures. Don't people explain Buddhist scriptures in India? You don't even seem to know."

Patriarch Bodhidharma replied, "The Sutra lectures in India explain the wordless true Sutra. The Sutras you lecture on here have words."

Dharma Master Shen Guang asked, "What is the wordless true Sutra?"

Patriarch Bodhidharma answered, "The Sutra I lecture is wordless. It is just a piece of blank paper. As to the Sutras you lecture, the inked areas are words, and the blank areas are paper. Why are you explaining them?"

Dharma Master Shen Guang replied, "I lecture on the Sutras to teach people how to end birth and death!"

Having Not Yet Ended Birth and Death, His Annoyance Turns to Rage

Patriarch Bodhidharma said, "Since you teach people how to end birth and death, tell me, how does one end birth and death? In the Sutra you are lecturing, the inked areas are words, and the blank areas are paper. What do you use to teach people how to end birth and death? Have you ended your own birth and death?"

Hearing that, Dharma Master Shen Guang was speechless and thought to himself, "The things this Indian says are outlandish. Is he a manifestation of a demon king? Otherwise, how could he be slandering the Triple Jewel like that?" Thereupon, his annoyance turned to rage, and he lost his temper, "I'm going to try you out, you demon king!"

Once His Temper Flares, in His Rage, He Strikes the Patriarch

You see! His lectures caused flowers to rain down from the heavens and golden lotuses to well up from the earth, and still he lost his temper! That's why I said Buddhism seemed to exist in China, and yet it did not. What happened when he lost his temper? What happened when he got angry? He grabbed his weapon. What weapon? His string of recitation beads. His beads weren't lightweight like these "stars and moon Bodhi" beads of mine. His recitation beads were made of iron! They were hard and sturdy. His recitation beads were designed to be used as a weapon in case he encountered weird entities, demons, ghosts, wolves, reptiles, tigers, or panthers. He could conveniently grab his recitation beads and attack. This time, encountering Patriarch Bodhidharma, who had dared to challenge him so, his wrath was extreme, like a combination of tidal wave, avalanche, and earthquake. As he whipped out his beads, he snapped, "You are slandering the Dharma!" and cracked Patriarch Bodhidharma across the mouth.

The Blow Breaks Teeth;
He Swallows Them with the Blood

Patriarch Bodhidharma was caught unprepared, because he never expected that Dharma Master Shen Guang would hit him. Although certified sages can penetrate others' thoughts, the Patriarch did not reflect in advance on what the Dharma Master might do. Although Patriarch Bodhidharma had some skill in the martial arts, he was caught off guard. It never occurred to him that the monk would make such a vicious attack; that being unable to reply, he would resort to brute force. As a result, the blow broke off two of Patriarch Bodhidharma's teeth.

What did Patriarch Bodhidharma do about the two broken teeth? Well, he was a sage, and there's a legend about the teeth of a patriarch—a certified sage—and what happens if they get broken and he spits them out onto the ground. It's said that if a sage's teeth are knocked loose and he spits them out on the ground, it won't rain for three years there.

Patriarch Bodhidharma thought, "Ai! If it doesn't rain for three years, just imagine how many people will starve! I have come to China to save beings, not to kill them!" And so Patriarch Bodhidharma did not let his teeth fall to the ground. Instead, he swallowed them, just as if he were eating a pancake. Well, pancakes aren't that hard—it was more like eating bones! He swallowed them and made his exit.

Therefore, in China, there is a saying that came from that incident, "If someone knocks out the teeth of an arhat, the arhat swallows them."

Enduring the Insult,
The Patriarch Leaves Silently

Having broken off two of the Patriarch's teeth, Dharma Master Shen Guang felt that he had won a real victory. Without saying a word, Patriarch Bodhidharma turned around and left. He did not fight back. Not at all! Foreigners are bound to be bullied. After all, he couldn't go to the government and file suit against Dharma Master Shen Guang for knocking out two of his teeth. Those who have left home have to be patient; how much more must a Patriarch forbear! After that happened, he just left and headed toward Henan.

A Parrot, Understanding Who He Is, Asks How to Escape the Cage

On the road, he met a parrot imprisoned in a wicker cage. However, this bird was much more intelligent than the Dharma Master Shen Guang. Recognizing that Bodhidharma was a patriarch, the bird chirped,

> He Who Intentionally came from the West
> Intentionally came from the West,
> What method is best, if you please,
> To escape this cage and leave?

Although Patriarch Bodhidharma hadn't been able to find any people who really understood who he was, this parrot definitely recognized him. He knew who he was.

Hearing the bird's plea for help, Bodhidharma was pleased and taught the bird an expedient method—a provisional, not a real, Dharma. He said,

> To escape the cage, to escape the cage;
> Stick out both legs; shut both eyes.
> That is the way to escape from the cage!

It was a secret, wonderful formula—a secret Dharma. It's for sure the Patriarch whispered it. He didn't say it so loudly as I am speaking now! He certainly must have used a very small voice: "To escape the cage...that is the way to escape from the cage!" He spoke softly like that. Why? If he had said it out loud so that others could hear him, then the method would not have worked. From this we can see how much trouble the Patriarch took to be kind.

The Smart Bird, Pretending to Be Dead, Cleverly Escapes the Cage

Mastering the method taught, the little bird chirped, "All right! Good method! Now I understand how to get out of the cage!" When the bird saw his owner approaching in the distance, he applied the expedient method. Sticking his legs out straight and closing his eyes, he waited for his owner to come close.

Every day when the owner came home, he always played with this bird that he was so fond of. Talking to it would cheer him up. And so, as usual, upon his return, he first went to check on his bird. But this time when he looked in the cage he was shocked. He practically burst into tears. Why? His little bird lay on the floor of the cage, unmoving. He couldn't have been more upset if his own son had died. In fact, it's likely that this bird meant even more to him than his son!

Freedom over Birth and Death Comes
When We Truly Escape Our Cage

The owner pulled open the cage door and gently placed the little bird in his hand. It was still warm, not yet cold. In fact, because the bird was only pretending to be dead, of course it retained its body warmth. The owner peeked at the little thing, turning his hand this way and that. The bird didn't even quiver. Whatever angle he viewed it from, the bird appeared to be really dead. Its body was still warm; only its breath seemed to have stopped. Slowly he open his hand... PHLLRTTPHLRTTPHLRTT! The bird broke loose from his hand and flew away! It had escaped from the cage!

But we are still in a cage right now! How do we escape? As to human beings, you shouldn't think you are free. Don't misinterpret freedom, saying, "I am really free. If I want to eat, I eat; if I want to drink alcohol, I drink alcohol. I can do anything I please. I can ignore the rules if I want to! That's what I call freedom!" That's a misinterpretation of freedom. To be truly free, you must be free of birth and death, and then if you wish to fly into space, you can fly into space; if you wish to burrow into the earth, you can burrow into the earth. If you can do that, you will gain the kind of freedom that the little bird gained.

47

The Yamas of the Ten Courts
Invite the Master to Tea

Dharma Master Shen Guang knocked out two of that Indian monk's teeth, and since the monk didn't retaliate, the Dharma Master figured he had the advantage—that he'd won the victory. He'd put a barbarian monk in his place. But not long after he struck the barbarian, the Yamas of the Ten Courts paid a call: "Dharma Master, your life is supposed to end today. We Yamas from the Ten Courts now wish to invite you to a meeting. We will go there to investigate your case."

Hearing that, Dharma Master Shen Guang exclaimed, "What?" as he watched those ten black-faced people who claimed to be the Yamas of the Ten Courts approach him and request his presence in the dark yin realm where he was to take tea with King Yama. Dharma Master Shen Guang said, "Oh! What? I still have to die? I also have to die?"

The Yamas of the Ten Courts challenged him, "Why would you not have to die? What talents do you have that make you think you don't have to die?"

Dharma Master Shen Guang replied, "I speak Sutras so well that flowers rain down from the heavens and golden lotuses well forth from the earth; doesn't that qualify me as having ended birth and death? I still have to die?"

The Yamas of the Ten Courts said, "Of course you have to die!"

49

Even the Venerable Yamas Will Bow to Whoever Is Free from Death

Dharma Master Shen Guang asked, "Who in this world is free from death? Is there anyone in this world who has really ended birth and death?"

"There is," the Yamas of the Ten Courts replied. "There's someone in this world who has ended birth and death."

"Who?" asked Dharma Master Shen Guang. "Please tell me so that I can follow him to learn the way to end birth and death."

The Yamas of the Ten Courts replied, "Which one? He is the black-faced monk whose teeth you knocked out. He is free from death. King Yama has no control over him. Not only that, King Yama bows in respect to him every day!"

Dharma Master Shen Guang replied, "Oh! He is a monk who has ended birth and death? Fine. I don't want to go with you yet. I want to go find that black-faced monk and follow him to learn the Dharma-door of ending birth and death. Could you wait a bit to take me away? Is that all right? I am determined to end birth and death! Could you speak to King Yama on my behalf to see if he can give me a little more time so I can go learn this Dharma-door?"

The Yamas of the Ten Courts replied, "All right. Since you are so sincere, what you ask is not beyond the realm of possibility. We can be expedient and agree to a compromise."

Well, they didn't drag him off to have tea with King Yama. You know, of course, that King Yama also enjoys a good cup of tea. You who like to drink tea should exercise some caution! Ha! Ha!

Pursuing the Patriarch,
He Follows Him Straight to Mount Song

As soon as Dharma Master Shen Guang heard that the Yamas of the Ten Courts agreed to his request, he was so delighted that he even forgot to put on his shoes. So anxious was he to avoid King Yama that he raced barefoot after Patriarch Bodhidharma.

Patriarch Bodhidharma walked on ahead; the Dharma Master pursued him from behind. In his pursuit, he passed the parrot who had gained his freedom through the help of Patriarch Bodhidharma. Suddenly he understood, "Oh! That's what it's all about! I have to play dead. I have to be a living dead person!"

Dharma Master Shen Guang raced after Patriarch Bodhidharma. The Patriarch paid no attention to him but just kept on walking. Dharma Master Shen Guang followed him all the way to Bear's Ear Mountain, close to Mount Song, the Central Yo [sacred mountain], near Luoyang. The Five Yo [sacred mountains] are Mount Tai (Peace) in the east, Mount Heng (Authority) in the south, Mount Hua (Elegance) in the west, Mount Heng (Constancy) in the north, and Mount Song (Eminence) in the center.

While the Patriarch Sits Facing the Rock Wall, The Dharma Master Seeks to Repent

He caught up with Patriarch Bodhidharma, only to find him sitting in meditation facing a rock wall. He was turned toward the wall and not speaking to anyone. Seeing the Patriarch there in meditation, the Dharma Master knelt down and did not get up, saying, "When I first saw you, I did not know that you were a patriarch, a sage. I hit you with my recitation beads, and I'm really sorry. I am truly remorseful. I know you are a person with true virtue. You are a noble one who cherishes the Way. I am now seeking the Way, the Dharma, from you."

Patriarch Bodhidharma took one look at him and said nothing; he remained sitting in meditation. The Dharma Master knelt there seeking the Dharma for nine years. Patriarch Bodhidharma meditated facing the wall for nine years, and Dharma Master Shen Guang knelt there for nine years.

We cultivators of the present time sit for a while and then begin to feel aches in our waist and pains in our legs, getting very uncomfortable. All of us should reflect on what it would be like to kneel for nine years. How comfortable would that be? How much fun?

All of us should reflect on how those of old could kneel for nine years seeking the Dharma. We of today can't endure nine days or even nine hours without feeling it's impossibly bitter and terribly uncomfortable. Some of us also think: "In the morning I don't get breakfast, and at night there's nothing sweet to drink." All sorts of such false thoughts arise. Comparing ourselves to those of old, how do we feel?

Do you feel concerned about Dharma Master Shen Guang? He knelt there for nine long years. Probably some of you are thinking, "Incredible! Kneeling for nine years like that, Dharma Master Shen Guang's legs must have really hurt. It must have been much

worse than the leg pain we experience sitting in meditation. Nine years is a long time." Someone else may say, "He must have run away." Let me tell you, he did not run away! If he had run away after he had knelt for nine years, all the effort he made would have been wasted. It would not have been worth a penny. Therefore, he would rather have knelt there until he died than to have run away. "Patriarch, if you don't transmit to me the Dharma for avoiding King Yama, I will not get up under any circumstances."

Kneeling for Nine Years,
He Seeks the Dharma for Ending Birth and Death

During the nine years he knelt there, Dharma Master Shen Guang's skill was almost perfected, but not quite. One year, it snowed very heavily on Bear's Ear Mountain. Outside, the snow was deep. Patriarch Bodhidharma sat meditating, and as Dharma Master Shen Guang knelt there, he became buried in snow up to his waist. Imagine that! The snow must have been at least two to three feet deep, yet Dharma Master Shen Guang continued to kneel there seeking the Dharma. At about lunch time, Patriarch Bodhidharma got up from where he had been facing the wall meditating and saw that the Dharma Master was still kneeling. He said, "What are you doing here, acting like that? It's snowing so hard. Why are you still kneeling there?"

Dharma Master Shen Guang replied, "I am seeking the Dharma! I am seeking the Way! Please, Patriarch, be compassionate and transmit to me the method for avoiding King Yama. Before, I lectured on the Sutras, but could not end my own birth and death. Now I want to end birth and death. Please, Patriarch, transmit the Dharma for ending birth and death to me."

Patriarch Bodhidharma thought for a while and said, "Now you are kneeling here pleading with me to teach you the Dharma for escaping King Yama. But do you remember the time when I asked you a question and you responded by breaking off two of my teeth with your recitation beads? Do you remember that time?" Then, he asked, "Is it snowing?"

Dharma Master Shen Guang said, "Yes, it is snowing. I am buried in snow up to my waist."

Patriarch Bodhidharma asked, "What color is the snow?"

Dharma Master Shen Guang said, "Snow is white, of course. Everyone knows that

59

snow is white. I am not the only one who says so."

Then Patriarch Bodhidharma gave him a problem to solve. He assigned him his test question. He said, "Fine. You see that the snow falling from the sky is white. When the fallen snow turns red, I will transmit the Dharma to you. I will teach you how to end birth and death and escape from King Yama. If there is no red fallen snow, you are out of luck. What a vicious monk you are to have knocked out two of my teeth with your recitation beads! I have already been most compassionate by not seeking revenge; how could I possibly transmit the Dharma to you!"

You all think about it: wouldn't solving that problem have been like trying to find a hair on a monk's head? In other words, wasn't it impossible? Monks are bald; there would be no hair to be found, right? But Patriarch Bodhidharma was searching for a hair on a monk's head. He said, "Whenever you see red fallen snow, then I will transmit the Dharma to you." That was the test question he gave to Dharma Master Shen Guang to answer.

The Fallen Snow Turns Red;
He Presents It to the Patriarch

The problem was stated and Dharma Master Shen Guang solved it. He wrote the essay. How did he solve the problem? He thought, "What a mess I'm in now! The fallen snow is white. How could it turn red?" Aha! He raised his head and saw a knife hanging from a rock. The knife was a cultivator's precept blade. It hung there in readiness in case the time ever came when the cultivator faced a situation in which he would be forced to break the precepts. In that case, he would rather use the knife to cut off his own head in order to preserve the integrity of his precept substance than to violate the precepts. When Dharma Master Shen Guang saw the knife, he had an idea. "Great! Since you want red snow, I will show you red snow." He took down the knife. Now, what do you suppose he was about to do? Was he going to kill Patriarch Bodhidharma? No. He grabbed the knife and with one swing cut off his own arm. That was how he solved the problem. He completed his essay.

He cut off his arm. What happened then? Well, blood gushed out of the wound, dyeing the snow red. A lot of blood flowed and he mixed the blood with the snow, dyeing the originally white snow red. Dharma Master Shen Guang took something, perhaps a bamboo basket, scooped up a basketful of red snow, and said, "Patriarch, please take a look: now the snow is red."

He Seeks the Dharma with a True Mind; the Patriarch Transmits It to Him

Patriarch Bodhidharma took a look, "Really? Ah! It really is red snow." Actually, the Patriarch had the intention of helping him; he just wanted to test his true mind.

Well, the Patriarch was moved and said, "I did not come to China for nothing, after all! I have met someone who seeks the Dharma with a true mind, to the point he could cut off his own arm for the sake of Dharma. He truly has a bit of sincerity! All right! I will transmit the Dharma to you."

Thus, the Patriarch taught him with the Dharma door of the mind-to-mind seal and certification. He taught him with a direct pointing to the human mind that would allow him to see the nature and realize Buddhahood. He taught him how to cultivate and how to apply effort. He said, "In China, you are the Second Patriarch," and transmitted to Dharma Master Shen Guang the Proper Dharma Eye Treasury, the Wonderful Mind of Nirvana.

Searching for His Mind, He Cannot Find It; His Mind Is Already Calmed

After Dharma Master Shen Guang listened to the Dharma, his arm began to hurt. A while ago, he hadn't thought about his arm; he only thought about how he could get the snow to turn red. He forgot all about the pain in his arm. But after Patriarch Bodhidharma had finished explaining the Dharma to him, his discursive mind became active again. "Oow! The stump of the arm I just cut off really hurts!" Then he said to Patriarch Bodhidharma, "Ouch! My mind is in pain. I can't stand it! Please, Patriarch, quiet my mind."

"Your mind is in pain?" said Patriarch Bodhidharma. "Bring out your mind and show it to me. Then I will help quiet it for you, and you won't feel any more pain."

Dharma Master Shen Guang searched for his mind. Where was his mind? He looked in the north, east, south, west, in the intermediate points, and up and down. It was simply not to be found anywhere! At last he said to Patriarch Bodhidharma, "I can't find my mind! It is nowhere to be found."

"I have already finished quieting your mind!" said the Patriarch. "You can't find your mind; I have already calmed it for you."

Upon hearing that, the Second Patriarch suddenly became enlightened. Those few words brought him to a great awakening. Having achieved a profound awakening, his mind no longer hurt, his liver did not hurt, nor did the tips of the hairs in his pores. From that time on, he cultivated the Dharma door taught by Patriarch Bodhidharma, known as "a direct pointing to the human mind that leads to seeing the nature and realizing Buddhahood; a special transmission beyond the teaching that is not set forth in words or language."

The Second Patriarch transmitted this Dharma door to the Third Patriarch, who

in turn passed it to the Fourth Patriarch. The Fourth Patriarch transmitted it to the Fifth Patriarch. The Fifth Patriarch then transmitted that Dharma to the Sixth Patriarch. That Dharma has been passed down from generation to generation in China. Now it has come to America. But here in America, no one has knelt for nine years, and no one needs to. All you have to do is to bring forth a true mind to cultivate; then you will be able to attain this Dharma.

At this point, if I wanted to discuss this Dharma, the meanings would be infinite and boundless. Those few words of Dharma that Patriarch Bodhidharma spoke to Dharma Master Shen Guang were ineffably wonderful. Let these few sentences suffice to describe the event:

> *The myriad dharmas return to the one; the one returns to unity.*
> *Shen Guang, having not yet understood, ran after Bodhidharma.*
> *At Bear's Ear Mountain he knelt before him for nine years,*
> *Seeking a little something to escape King Yama.*

The myriad dharmas return to the one; the one returns to unity. Ten thousand dharmas return to one. It's said that:

> *A single source disperses into a myriad differences.*
> *A myriad differences return to a single source.*

Well, if the myriad dharmas return to one, where does the one return? And how does the one become unity? The character for unity (合) is composed of a person (人), the number one (一), and a mouth (口). Beneath the person is a one, and beneath the one is a mouth. Put together, they make unity. In cultivation, we should cultivate one Dharma door. The myriad dharmas return to the one; the one returns to unity. Unity

can also be equated with zero (◯).

Shen Guang, having not yet understood, ran after Bodhidharma. At first, Dharma Master Shen Guang did not understand the meaning of unity, and so he pursued Patriarch Bodhidharma.

At Bear's Ear Mountain he knelt before him for nine years. Not to speak of nine years, we can't even manage to kneel for nine hours.

Seeking a little something to escape King Yama. All he wanted was for Patriarch Bodhidharma to point out something to him; he wanted to know how to cultivate, how to be able to end birth and death and get out of the cycle of rebirth. He wanted to know how to get beyond King Yama's jurisdiction. That's what he wanted.

This has been a description of some of the events that transpired when Dharma Master Shen Guang encountered Patriarch Bodhidharma. Once before when I spoke this public record, a child who heard it was delighted and asked me, "During the nine years Dharma Master Shen Guang knelt, did he eat or not?"

The child thought up a question about eating probably because he liked to eat and was afraid of getting hungry. If he didn't fear getting hungry, he could also try kneeling for nine years. Anyway, he first had to ask if the Dharma Master got to eat while he knelt for nine years.

I replied, "Of course he ate! How could anyone go nine years without eating and still live? When it was time to eat he could get up and eat. When he needed to relieve himself, he could get up and relieve himself. When the Patriarch ate, he ate, too. When the Patriarch meditated, he knelt. It's true he knelt for nine years seeking the Dharma. It's just that the records don't give all the details of his lifestyle."

Poison Cannot Invade the Body of a Sage

While Patriarch Bodhidharma was in China, people attempted to poison him six times. Who poisoned him? It was Bodhiruchi, also called Vinaya Master Guang Tong, the same Small Vehicle Dharma Master who forced the Patriarch's two disciples out of China. He was extremely jealous of Patriarch Bodhidharma. He prepared a vegetarian meal and offered it to the Patriarch. The problem was, he laced the food with a lethal poison. Anyone would have died from the dose. Well, did the Patriarch Bodhidharma know that the food was poisoned? He knew! Although he knew it was poisoned, he ate it anyway. After he ate it, he asked someone to bring him a tray, and then he vomited the food onto the tray. The poison he vomited was transformed into a pile of writhing snakes. That was the first time.

After that unsuccessful attempt, Dharma Master Bodhiruchi couldn't figure out why the Patriarch had not been poisoned to death. The second time he doubled the dose of poison. It hadn't worked the previous time; this time he used more poison. He even used a more lethal variety to try to poison the Patriarch. Again, Patriarch Bodhidharma ate the food. Then he sat atop a huge boulder and relieved nature. The force of the poison that was eliminated exploded on the boulder, breaking not only the potency of the poison but also splitting the boulder as well. That was the second time.

Having Transmitted the Dharma to Someone, He Appears to Enter Nirvana

After that there was a third, fourth, fifth, and sixth time. Each of those six times, he ingested the poison. One day, Patriarch Bodhidharma said to Dharma Master Shen Guang, "I came to China because I saw that here were people and other beings with a propensity for the Great Vehicle. That is why I brought the Great Vehicle Buddhadharma to China. Now I have already transmitted the Dharma to someone who will continue the line. I am not going to stay here any longer. I am ready to die now."

Great Master Hui Ke (Dharma Master Shen Guang) asked Patriarch Bodhidharma, "In India, did you transmit the Dharma to your disciples? Did you also give the robe and the bowl as certification?"

"I transmitted the Dharma in India," replied Bodhidharma, "but I did not use the robe and the bowl as a token of faith. That is because the people of India are straightforward. When they cultivate and attain the fruition, they know they must be certified. If no one certifies them, they do not say, 'I have attained the Way! I have certified to the fruition! I have given proof to Arhatship! I am a Bodhisattva!' They do not speak like that. People there are upright and straight.

"Chinese people, however, are different. In China there are many beings with a propensity for the Great Vehicle, but there are also many people who lie. Having not yet cultivated to successful completion, such people claim to have the Way. Having not yet certified to the fruition, such people claim to be certified sages. That is why the robe and bowl must be used here as a token of certification. Therefore I will transmit the robe and bowl to prove that you have received the transmission. Guard them well and take care."

With the transmission of the Dharma from Patriarch Bodhidharma, Dharma

Master Shen Guang received the name Hui Ke, which means "Able Wisdom," evidence that his wisdom was truly up to the task; it was sufficient. Dharma Master Shen Guang, that is, Great Master Hui Ke, listened to Patriarch Bodhidharma's instructions and thereupon understood the Dharma transmission he had received.

As He Returns West Carrying One Shoe, He Encounters Song Yun

Patriarch Bodhidharma then pretended to enter Nirvana. People buried his coffin and thought the matter was finished. However, right at that time, a diplomatic representative from Northern Wei called Song Yun met Patriarch Bodhidharma in the vicinity of the Qin Range on the road to Zhongnan Mountain. When they met, Patriarch Bodhidharma was carrying one shoe in his hand. He said to Song Yun, "The king of your country died today. Your country is in turmoil. Return quickly! There is work to be done."

Song Yun thought, "Nothing is happening in my country." Then he asked Patriarch Bodhidharma, "Great Master, where are you going then?"

"Back to India," he replied.

"Great Master, to whom did you transmit your Dharma?"

Patriarch Bodhidharma replied, "In China after forty years, there will be someone able ('Ke')." "Able" was a reference to Great Master Hui Ke.

79

His Prediction Was True:
The Emperor Had Died

Song Yun returned to his country, Northern Wei, and relayed this matter, "A couple of days ago when I was traveling along the Qin Range near Mount Zhongnan, I met Patriarch Bodhidharma. He was carrying a shoe in his hand. I asked where he was heading, and he said he was going back to India. He told me the day I met him that our Emperor had died. Now I have come back and found that it did happen on that very day. How did he know? Patriarch Bodhidharma's words are really efficacious."

Only One Shoe in an Empty Coffin: Where Is the Patriarch?

Those who heard his tale retorted, "Patriarch Bodhidharma? You must have seen a ghost! Patriarch Bodhidharma is already dead. He was buried in such and such a place. How could you have met him?" No one believed Song Yun's story. "He is already dead, how could you have met him? Let's go together and dig up his grave." When they arrived at the grave, they said, "He had already been dead a long time when you say you saw him. Is it possible that he did not die after all?" So they dug up Patriarch Bodhidharma's grave and opened the coffin. It was empty. There was nothing inside but one shoe. Since Patriarch Bodhidharma had taken one shoe with him, only one shoe remained in the coffin.

Well, where did Patriarch Bodhidharma go? No one knows. Perhaps he came to America. It's not for sure. But no one would recognize him, because he can change his appearance at will. He goes through thousands of transformations and a myriad changes according to his convenience. When he reached China he said he was one hundred and fifty years old, and when he left he said he was still one hundred and fifty years old. Where did he go? No one knows. You may suggest that we look it up in the historical records, but no historical references can be found. This has been a general discussion of Patriarch Bodhidharma's life in China.

As the Sixth Patriarch Washes His Sash, Fang Bian Relates a Strange Tale

In the *Sixth Patriarch's Platform Sutra* is a passage that mentions how one day when the Sixth Patriarch was in the mountain forest washing the sash which he received from the Fifth Patriarch, a monk came and bowed to him. After paying his respects, the monk said, "My name is Fang Bian. I am a native of Sichuan. A few days ago, I saw Patriarch Bodhidharma in South India. He told me to come back here to the Land of Tang [China]. The Patriarch said, 'From Great Kashyapa onward to me and down through the generations, the Proper Dharma Eye Treasury has been transmitted along with the Patriarch's robe, the twenty-five piece sash—the sanghati. It is now in China, having been transmitted to the sixth generation who is at Cao Creek of Shaoguan. Go quickly to that place and pay obedience to the Sixth Patriarch!'"

Think about it. The First Patriarch Bodhidharma already died in China, but this monk Fang Bian met him in India during the Sixth Patriarch's time. Is it not strange? Actually, it's not that surprising, because up to now, no one knows where Patriarch Bodhidharma has gone.

Filial Son Wang Practiced Filiality
Beside the Grave for Six Years

Speaking of that, I recall another true incident I would like to relate to you. This is no tale, it's a true story.

When I was in Manchuria there were several causes and conditions which inspired me to cultivate the Way. The person whom I admired the most in Manchuria was Filial Son Wong. He started his filial period of mourning when he was twenty-eight. It gets very cold in Manchuria. He used wooden boards and nails to build a small hut, but it didn't keep out the bitter cold. He lived there for three years and then continued the filial mourning period for another three years. He spent six years there altogether. During the last year, he did not talk to anyone, no matter who came to visit him. Every day he sat in that small hut either meditating or reciting sutras. He recited the *Vajra Sutra*.

At the End of His Filial Mourning,
a Dharma Protector Presented a Sage

When his last three years of mourning were almost over, he had a false thought, "Mount Qian (Thousand) and Mount Guangning (Expansive Tranquility) are two famous mountains in Manchuria. In those two mountains, many thousand-year-old Bhikshus are cultivating. After I complete this mourning period, I also will go there to cultivate the Way."

Two days after he had that false thought, while he was sitting in meditation, he heard a Dharma Protector say to him, "Today a nobleman will come to visit you." When he heard that a nobleman was coming, he assumed it would be a high official of some kind. He just waited.

A Monk from the Ming Dynasty
Came to Visit during the Republic

He waited till a little past ten and saw a monk wearing a tattered robe and carrying a stick with a bundle attached that held his clothing and bedding. The monk put down his bundle and spoke to him. Now, Filial Son Wong wasn't talking, but he mentally asked the monk, "Where did you come from?" He spoke with his mind, not his mouth.

The monk answered, saying, "I come from Mount Guangning."

Filial Son Wong asked, "What is your name? What are you called?"

The monk replied, "My name? Well, are you familiar with the Ming Dynasty? I was a general during the Ming Dynasty. Later, I left home and started cultivating the Way. Recently, I have felt that I have some affinities with you, so I have come here today to see you." He also said, "I know you are thinking of going to Mount Guangning to cultivate. That is a place for people who only take care of their own virtue in solitude. As for you, you should take care of the whole world. Your affinity with people in this place is very strong. Don't go to Mount Guangning. After you finish your period of filial mourning, stay here and build a monastery. It would be best to propagate the Buddhadharma here." After saying those few sentences to Filial Son Wong, the monk left.

That monk claimed that he was from the Ming Dynasty. How can we prove what he said was true? The fact that he knew the question asked in Filial Son Wong's mind proved that he was a person who had already attained the penetration of knowing others' thoughts--a state associated with the Five Eyes and Six Spiritual Powers. However, Filial Son Wong lived during the Republic, about three hundred years after the Ming Dynasty. Over three hundred years had passed, and yet this monk was still alive and came to visit Filial Son Wong. This incident proves the claim that someone

saw Patriarch Bodhidharma in India a few hundred years after he entered the stillness, and that the situation described by Fang Bian regarding the transmission of the sash, are not that unusual. Those incidences were, in fact, rather ordinary occurrences; not all that strange. The inconceivable states of Patriarch Bodhidharma will never be forgotten. The Chinese people will forever remember Patriarch Bodhidharma.

He Transmitted the Dharma to Three People;
His Body Is Empty and Gone

After the Patriarch transmitted the Dharma to Great Master Hui Ke, he also accepted many other Chinese disciples. While he sat facing the wall for nine years at Bear's Ear Mountain, it's not known how many people came to take refuge, pay their respects, and bow to him as their teacher. Among them were three individuals whom Patriarch Bodhidharma mentioned when he was about to pass into stillness. He said, "I came to China and transmitted my Dharma to three people. One received my marrow, one received my bones, and one received my flesh." That is why he himself had no physical body left. He had divided his body up and given it away to others.

Great Master Hui Ke received Patriarch Bodhidharma's marrow. Chan Master Dao Yu received Patriarch Bodhidharma's bones. The third was Bhikshuni Zong Chi (Dao Ji). Do you remember her? When I lectured on the *Dharma Flower Sutra* didn't I tell you about how a blue lotus flower grew from her mouth after she died? That Bhikshuni received Patriarch Bodhidharma's flesh. She consumed Patriarch Bodhidharma's flesh, Dhyana Master Dao Yu chewed up Patriarch Bodhidharma's bones, and Patriarch Hui Ke drank Patriarch Bodhidharma's marrow. In the end, Patriarch Bodhidharma had no body at all. And so don't look for him in America; you won't find him.

 **The Dharma Realm Buddhist Association**

The Dharma Realm Buddhist Association (DRBA) was founded in the United States of America in 1959 by the Venerable Master Hsuan Hua [prior to his own arrival in the U.S.]to bring the genuine teachings of the Buddha to the entire world. Its goals are to propagate the Proper Dharma, to translate the Mahayana Buddhist scriptures into the world's languages and to promote ethical education. The members of the association guide themselves with six ideals established by the Venerable Master which are: no fighting, no greed, no seeking, no selfishness, no pursuing personal advantage, and no lying. They hold in mind the credo:

> *Freezing, we do not scheme.*
> *Starving, we do not beg.*
> *Dying of poverty, we ask for nothing.*
> *According with conditions, we do not change.*
> *Not changing, we accord with conditions.*
> *We adhere firmly to our three great principles.*
> *We renounce our lives to do the Buddha's work.*
> *We take responsibility in molding our own destinies.*
> *We rectify our lives to fulfill our role as members of the Sangha.*
> *Encountering specific matters, we understand the principles.*
> *Understanding the principles, we apply them in specific matters.*
> *We carry on the single pulse of the patriarchs' mind-transmission.*

The Dharma Realm Buddhist Association

During the following decades, international Buddhist communities such as Gold Mountain Monastery, the City of Ten Thousand Buddhas, the City of the Dharma Realm and various other branch facilities were founded. All these operate under the traditions of the Venerable Master and through the auspices of the Dharma Realm Buddhist Association. Following the' guidelines of Shakyamuni Buddha, the Sangha members in these monastic facilities maintain the practices of taking only one meal a day and of always wearing their precept sashes. Reciting the Buddha's name, studying the teachings, and practicing meditation, they dwell together in harmony and personally put into practice the Buddha's teachings. Reflecting Master Hua's emphasis on translation and education, the Association also sponsors an International Translation Institute, vocational training programs for Sangha and laity, Dharma Realm Buddhist University, and elementary and secondary schools.

The Way-places of this Association are open to sincere individuals of all races, religions, and nationalities. Everyone who is willing to put forth his/her best effort in nurturing humaneness, righteousness, merit, and virtue in order to understand the mind and see the nature is welcome to join in the study and practice.

Venerable Master Hsuan Hua
The Founder of Dharma Realm Buddhist Association

The Venerable Master Hsuan Hua was also known as An Tse and To Lun. The name Hsuan Hua was bestowed upon him after he received the transmission of the Wei Yang Lineage of the Chan School from Venerable Elder Hsu Yun. He left the home life at the age of nineteen. After the death of his mother, he lived in a tiny thatched hut by her grave-side for three years, as an act of filial respect. During that time, he practiced meditation and studied the Buddha's teachings. Among his many practices were eating only once a day at midday and never lying down to sleep.

In 1948 the Master arrived in Hong Kong, where he founded the Buddhist Lecture Hall and other monasteries. In 1962 he brought the Proper Dharma to America and the West, where he lectured extensively on the major works of the Mahayana Buddhist canon and established the Dharma Realm Buddhist Association, as well as the City of Ten Thousand Buddhas, the International Translation Institute, various other monastic facilities, Dharma Realm Buddhist University, Developing Virtue Secondary School, Instilling Goodness Elementary school, the vocational Sangha and Laity Training Programs, and other education centers.

The Master passed into stillness on June 7, 1995, in Los Angeles, U.S.A., causing many people throughout the world to mourn the sudden setting of the sun of wisdom. Although he has passed on, his lofty example will always be remembered. Throughout his life he worked selflessly and vigorously to benefit the people of the world and all living beings. His wisdom and compassion inspired many to correct their faults and lead wholesome lives.

Here we include the Records of the Mendicant of Chang Bai written by the Venerable Master to serve as a model for all of us to emulate.

The Mendicant of Chang Bai was simple and honest in nature.

He was always quick to help people and benefit others.

Forgetting himself for the sake of the Dharma,

he was willing to sacrifice his life.

Bestowing medicines according to people's illnesses,

he offered his own marrow and skin.

His vow was to unite in substance with millions of beings.

His practice exhausted empty space as he gathered in the myriad potentials,

Without regard for past, future, or present;

With no distinctions of north, south, east, or west.

Namo Dharma Protector Wei Tuo Bodhisattva

Verse of Transference

May the merit and virtue accrued from this work
Adorn the Buddhas' Pure Lands,
Repaying the four kinds of kindness above
And aiding those suffering in the paths below.
May those who see and hear of this
All bring forth the resolve for Bodhi
And, when this retribution body is over,
Be born together in the Land of Ultimate Bliss.

Commentary on Buddhist Sutras
by Ven. Master Hua's

	Price US
Amitabha Sutra	$8.00
Dharma Flower (Lotus) Sutra (1 set, 10 books)	$79.50
The Wonderful Dharma Lotus Flower Sutra (Vol. 11-16)	@$.10.00
Flower Adornment (Avatamsaka) Sutra (1 set, 22 books)	$174.50
Flower Adornment (Avatamsaka) Sutra Prologue (1set, 4 books)	$38.00
Heart Sutra & Verses Without a Stand	$7.50
Medicine Master Sutra (softcover)	$10.00
Shurangama Sutra (1 set, 7 books)	$59.50
Shurangama Sutra, Vol.8: The Fifty Skandha-Demon States	$20.00
Great Strength Bodhisattva's Perfect Penetration	$5.00
Shastra on the Door to Understanding the Hundred Dharmas	$6.50
Sixth Patriarch Sutra (hardcover)	$15.00
Sixth Patriarch Sutra (softcover)	$10.00
Sutra In Forty-two Sections	$5.00
Sutra of the Past Vows of Earth Store Bodhisattva (hardcover, commentary)	$16.00
Song of Enlightenment	$5.00
Vajra Prajna Paramita (Diamond) Sutra	$8.00
Sutra of the Past Vows of Earth Store Bodhisattva (softcover, sutra text only)	$5.00

Flower Adornment (Avatamsaka) Sutra
A Basic Explanation by Venerable Master Hua

Known as the "King of Kings" of all Buddhist scriptures because of its profundity and great length (81 rolls containing more than 700,000 Chinese characters), this Sutra contains the most complete explanation of the Buddha's state and the Bodhisattva's quest for Awakening.

. . . .

Dharma Flower (Lotus) Sutra
A Basic Explanation by Venerable Master Hua

In this Sutra, which was spoken during the last period of the Buddha's teaching, the Buddha proclaims the ultimate principles of the Dharma, which unite all previous teachings into one. The entire work comprises sixteen volumes.

**Shurangama Sutra:
The Fifty Skandha Demon States**
A Basic Explanation by Venerable Master Hua

A bilingual (Chinese/English) edition of Venerable Master Hua's commentary on the final section of the Shurangama Sutra (volume eight of the English only edition). Essential reading for anyone who practices meditation or who wishes to follow a spiritual teacher.

**Sutra of the Past Vows of
Earth Store Bodhisattva**
A Basic Explanation by Venerable Master Hua

This Sutra tells how Earth Store Bodhisattva (Kshitigarbha) attained his position among the greatest Bodhisattvas as the Foremost in Vows. It also explains the workings of karma, how beings undergo rebirth, and the various kinds of hells. This is the first English translation.

Medicine Master Sutra
A Basic Explanation by Venerable Master Hua

This sutra describes Medicine Master (Akshobhya) Vaidurya Light Thus Come One's twelve great vows, the benefits derived from hearing this sutra, how to worship the Buddha and uphold the sutra, the benefits from worshipping and upholding, and twelve yaksha generals who repay Medicine Master Buddha's kindness.

. . . .

Sixth Patriarch's Sutra
A Basic Explanation by Venerable Master Hua

One of the foremost scriptures of Ch'an Buddhism, this text describes the life and teachings of the remarkable Patriarch of the T'ang Dynasty, Great Master Hui Neng, who, though unable to read or write, was enlightened to the true nature of all things.

DHARMA REALM BUDDHIST ASSOCIATION
CITY OF TEN THOUSAND BUDDHAS

P.O.Box 217, 2001 Talmage Road, Talmage, CA 95481-0217 U.S.A.
Tel: (707) 462-0939   Fax: (707) 462-0949

. . . .

The International Translation Institute
1777 Murchison Drive, Burlingame,
CA 94010-4504 U.S.A.
Tel: (650) 692-5912   Fax: (650) 692-5056

Institute for World Religions
(at Berkeley Buddhist Monastery)
2304 McKinley Avenue, Berkeley, CA 94703 U.S.A.
Tel: (510) 848-3440   Fax: (510) 548-4551

Gold Mountain Monastery
800 Sacramento Street, San Francisco, CA 94108 U.S.A.
Tel: (415) 421-6117   Fax: (415) 788-6001

Gold Sage Monastery
11455 Clayton Road, San Jose, CA 95127 U.S.A.
Tel: (408) 923-7243   Fax: (408) 923-1064

The City of the Dharma Realm
1029 West Capitol Avenue,
West Sacramento, CA 95691 U.S.A.
Tel/Fax: (916) 374-8268

Gold Wheel Monastery
235 North Avenue 58, Los Angeles, CA 90042 U.S.A.
Tel/Fax: (323) 258-6668

Long Beach Monastery
3361 East Ocean Boulevard, Long Beach, CA 90803 U.S.A.
Tel/Fax: (562) 438-8902

Blessings, Prosperity, and Longevity Monastery
4140 Long Beach Boulevard, Long Beach, CA 90807 U.S.A.
Tel/Fax: (562) 595-4966

Avatamsaka Hermitage
11721 Beall Mountain Road, Potomac,
MD 20854-1128 U.S.A.
Tel/Fax: (301) 299-3693

Gold Summit Monastery
233 First Avenue West, Seattle, WA 98119 U.S.A.
Tel/Fax: (206) 217-9320

Gold Buddha Monastery
248 E. 11th Avenue, Vancouver, B.C. V5T 2C3 Canada
Tel/Fax: (604) 709-0248

Avatamsaka Monastery
1009 Fourth Avenue S.W., Calgary, AB T2P 0K8 Canada
Tel/Fax: (403) 234-0644

Dharma Realm Buddhist Books
Distribution Society
11th Floor, 85 Chung-hsiao E. Road, Sec. 6,
Taipei, R.O.C.
Tel: (02) 2786-3022, 2786-2474   Fax: (02) 2786-2674

Dharma Realm Sage Monastery
20, Tung-hsi Shan-chuang, Hsing-lung Village, Liu-kuei,
Kaohsiung County, Taiwan, R.O.C.
Tel: (07) 689-3713   Fax: (07) 689-3870

Amitabha Monastery
7, Su-chien-hui, Chih-nan Village, Shou-feng,
Hualien County, Taiwan, R.O.C.
Tel: (03) 865-1956 Fax:(03) 865-3426

Guan Yin Sage Monasteryt (Tze Yun Tung)
Batu 5 1/2, Jalan Sungai Besi, Salak Selatan,
57100 Kuala Lumpur, Malaysia
Tel: (03)782-6560   Fax:(03) 780-1272

Kun Yam Thong (Deng Bi An Temple)
161, Jalan Ampang, 50450 Kuala Lumpur, Malaysia
Tel: (03) 2164-8055   Fax: (03)2163-7118

Lotus Vihara
136, Jalan Sekolah, 45600 Batang Berjuntai,
Selangor Darul Ehsan, Malaysia
Tel: (03) 3271-9439

Buddhist Lecture Hall
31 Wong Nei Chong Road, Top Floor,
Happy Valley, Hong Kong, China
Tel/Fax: 2572-7644